OF WATER NEVER CEASING

Praise for **KRISTIN ENTLER**

"A lyrical, unflinching debut that explores survival, chronic illness, and the fierce beauty of being alive. Through a knowing voice that blends vivid imagery, fragmented forms, prose poetry, and experimental structures, Entler captures life lived 'on a razor's edge,' where 'you will not die because you are sick but because you are alive.' Her poems move from hospital rooms to coastal shores, finding meaning in impermanece, isolation, nature, and endurance—'nature makes it look easy, all this dying...finding another way to make use of what's already gone.' This collection is both hymn and reckoning."

—Kelly Riedesel, *Proud Roads*

"In *Of Water Never Ceasing*, the body becomes a meeting ground for carrion and sweetgum, antibiotics and insulin. Some of the best moments in the collection push readers to just look at the world as it is: at the branch-grazed wings of insects, at kudzu and ivy, at rain-covered lichen. I loved this."

—Garrett Ashley, *Habitats* and *A Field Guide to North American Trees*

"*Of Water Never Ceasing* is a luminous meditation on chronic illness and life's unavoidable bounty, opening with a 'semi-overcast sky,' its clouds 'like stitches / holding closed someone else's fresh and sterile wounds.' Rooted in oak leaves and magnolias, rat snakes and kudzu, the long sway from Muscle Shoals to Mobile, Entler vines her wildly creative use of form with vibrant imagery and devastating observations. These poems invite us into a deeper listening to both the natural world and to each other."

—Candice M. Kelsey, *Another Place Altogether*

"Pearls & nurses. Phlegm & honey. A body leaning in the doorway of mythos. Like a southern accent that lingers, Entler's words are subtle in their staying power. We see & thus embrace ourselves in their naming of shared ghosts."

—Brody Parrish Craig, *The Patient Is an Unreliable Historian*

"With fierce lyric attention, the poems in Kristin Entler's debut collection, *Of Water Never Ceasing*, claim but won't define a queer body shaped by chronic illness. Entler confronts the insulting, diminishing language that frames disability narratives as 'such an inspiration.' This book rejects 'twisted empathy,' sanitization, and shame in favor of real, lived complexity. 'It's not special / to need clean air,' the poet writes, 'it is / normal to crave loving arms.'"

—Lauren Goodwin Slaughter, *Spectacle*

"Kristin Entler's *Of Water Never Ceasing* is a testament not only to disabled survival, but disabled futurity. These poems are bold and beautiful, acknowledgements of difficulty without relying on stereotypes or giving in to despair. This collection is an absolute force of a debut, and Entler is a stunning, necessary new voice for Southern and Disabled poetry."

—Raye Hendrix, *What Good Is Heaven*

"*Of Water Never Ceasing* is an air-hungry book, insistent on keeping the chronically ill body full of its own sovereign knowing. Entler's powerful poems have weathered hard waits inside of 'diagnoses's mouth' and surfaced 'full of wild,' offering moving antidotes against loneliness and 'more magic / than the meds.' Bless this new, essential voice."

—Geffrey Davis, *One Wild Word Away*

"These extraordinary poems hold a world where 'everything / is improbable,' and life exists on 'a razor's edge.' Kristin Entler possesses both a naturalist's powers of precise observation and a poet's mastery of metaphor. A compassionate and courageous book—and a beautiful one."

—Davis McCombs, *Lore*

⁂

"Entler vividly renders the natural beauty of Alabama with the experience of being fiercely alive in a chronically ill body. These are poems of endurance and urgency. *Of Water Never Ceasing* meditates on what it means to feel at home in a body, in a landscape, in the natural world."

—Ansel Elkins, *Blue Yodel*

⁂

"These lush, haunting poems describe living with a chronic illness, a kind of living that feels like drowning. The body isn't a refuge but a cage, yet the poems teem with life: bees and cicadas, pine and cypress. These poems celebrate a world that is vibrantly, gorgeously alive."

—Juliana Gray, *Honeymoon Palsy*

⁂

"*Of Water Never Ceasing* centers the disabled body as it travels worn paths of pain, treatment, enervation, and joy-seeking. Entler braids the natural world into poems about chronic illness that ring with marvel and frustration, desire and fear. 'Nature makes it look easy, // all this dying.' Entler takes us to 'the pause // between breaths' with this stunning debut."

—Rachel Mennies, *The Naomi Letters*

OF WATER NEVER CEASING

LOBLOLLY PRESS ASHEVILLE, NC

KRISTIN ENTLER

Published by Loblolly Press
loblollypress.com
Asheville, NC

Book design by Andrew Mack

Instagram: @loblolly_press
Newsletter: loblollypress.substack.com

Paperback ISBN: 979-8-9943089-1-2
Printed in the United States of America

First Printing, June 2026

CONTENTS

for my disabled community,
but especially my Nana

OF WATER NEVER CEASING

Oh how time hangs and drags till our aid comes!

—Dante Alighieri
Dante's Inferno trans. Allen Mandelbaum

ON BEING BORN A LUNGFISH

not all monsters are evil.
Omnivorous, sure. But hunger
does not mean spite

or vengeance or oppression;
just survival. Benign.
I'll digest myself

if it means waking up
to summer. A mucus
cocoon outside the body

makes more sense
than the internal membranes
drowning mammals alive.

Prehistoric as in stubborn,
as in evolution despite
the odds: five to one.

One in four on a Punnett
Square. Estivation.
Endangered fossil,

as in protected
as in scientists study
my respiratory system

my primitive limbs
how I survive in the crater
of an elephant's footprint

for what feels like endless
years; this dry season
of lonely metabolism.

THE GIRL WITH A PEARL IN HER WRIST

Where the bones meet. Right there below the pinkie's metacarpal line. She knows it is a pearl because the doctors told her so. A baroque pearl, according to her medical charts, though notations read that this is a best guess. That the only way to know the anatomy of the joint composite would be to biopsy. Every doctor so far recommends she let them prod her tender ligaments; she has always refused. It would be an invasive vanity procedure and after, she would no longer hold her body's final secret for herself. When cradled in the palm of her left hand, she can feel its glow like a fevered wound. Some nights, her body gives in to this insomnia. Drawn to the duneline empty handed, she carves a hole only she can fit and, without apology, accepts what she cannot change—

hot white thunder moon
sargassum blooms still soggy
tide swallows body

SONG FOR GENETIC ILLNESS AND IMAGINED PARENTAL GUILT

after *Song* by Brigit Pegeen Kelley

Listen: when she was born, they were told she was fine. Was
just a preemie. But six months old and their child only the size
of a wombfresh bundle, they knew something wasn't right. The
name of her ghost arrives—after months of searching for
the right person to look at the right organ, run the right test—
in a hazel-eyed-physician's broad, pink mouth: cystic fibrosis.
And all at once she's lucky to see the age of ten, then thirteen;
eighteen; twenty; thirty-three. A median age is never a promise.
He says it's what's caused her failure to thrive. He calls it that.
They know only that she's too small, has never put on weight
right. That every day of her still-short life, they've held her tiny
body over an open garbage bag as she throws up all the milk
she'd drunk the day before. She falls back asleep. No use watching
her breathe, they turn to the sun crowning its rays like a prayer
over the stand of long-leaf pines at the edge of the lake. With
each new study comes hope in the form of scientific evidence:
they only need to keep her alive long enough for science to catch
up to this body that is no one's fault. The doctors' words hardly cut
through the fugueshock. But there's a nurse who puts her hand on
their shoulders. Her hair makes her look like a young John Lennon
and she promises with her swimming pool eyes that their daughter
can be okay. It's a slim comfort in the face of an infant coughing
as hard as the full-grown adult they know she likely won't be able
to become and the first time they hear the word disabled, it drips
like honey down the nursery walls, a palpable grief for a future
when it'll be their job to make joy for the disappointment she has
in her own body. They'll promise her it's temporary, that she only
has to hang on long enough for science to figure out how to fix
her mutated genes she knows they're sorry to have passed down.

SIXTY-FIVE ROSES :|: CYSTIC FIBROSIS

"These sixty-five roses are dedicated to the people who continue to give unselfishly in the fight against cystic fibrosis."

– Cystic Fibrosis Foundation Blanket Embroidery

slime explodes green :|: pools
a slug stuck under my tongue
                    taste bacteria

bronchospasm :|: hacks
my mom calls
it   my seal-cough

when she calls the nurse
cough again :|:   ribs   constrict
airbags fight muscle

heating pads and ice
the nurse says, for the rib pain,
          antibiotics

as in plural :|: this time
:|:   *come in if this doesn't work*
in the next few days.

moldslime slips through :|: lips
on :|:   blanket across my lap.
smear phlegm on tissue

too late. Pastel stained
the knit :|: a permanent sick
hue :|: spot   still there

from the days before
I knew how to pronounce :|: all
my diagnoses   names

    that thin and woven
promise of :|: comfort I was
    small enough:|: to trust in

HOW OFTEN WE DESERVE BETTER THAN WE GET

A semi-overcast sky, the clouds cross like stitches
holding closed someone else's fresh and sterile wounds.
We give thanks it's not us in a hospital room tonight

and when you put it that way, shame seems silly.
The fall of oak leaves settles with the wind at moonrise
and anyways, distraction is an effective way to cope

with all kinds of hurt. Another day gone. There's no me
I've found that makes sense in this city. The horizon dark
as an alligator's leathery back. All that matters is where we are

right now: on a denim-blue couch, honey-crisp
laughs bursting from our throats in the early like magnolias,
a pink I haven't heard since this last spring's thaw.

WHY I CRINGE WHEN I HEAR MY NAME

because at 22 my schedule is set by the needle pumping meds into my chest.
because at 18 another therapist says I have no stable sense of self.
because at 14 a boy I kiss writes me a eulogy.
because at 10 I know dependency on a nurse's capability to thread veins.
because at 6 I'm calloused by family and friends twisting empathy into pity:

into *I would never want your life.*
into *I would just give up.*
into *such an inspiration.*
into *I shouldn't complain to you.*
into *you poor thing.*
into *bless your heart.*
into *I'd rather just die.*

as if turning off pain is that simple. as in just die.
as if I don't have any reason to stick around. as if a burden.
as if my name becomes worthless in my diagnoses's mouth.
as in there is no cure. as in chronic. as in until death.
as in the doctor who told my mom to just try again.
as in a child can only ever be what you tell them they are. as in just die.
as in I have only ever heard my name uttered in the past tense.
as in even though it was only for a short while, I'm glad to have known you.
as if my name was ever meant for anything besides a eulogy.

AFTER "POMPEII: TALES FROM AN ERUPTION," BIRMINGHAM MUSEUM OF ART, 2007

Sulfides, dioxides,
ash, and spewed smog

suffocated
Burning Dog
into a crisp comma.

Scorched skeletons,
cast and curated

from negative
space, their mouths agape.
No one thought

to notice the sputtering
respiration.

How do I write about
something no one notices?
About breathing?

About the pause

between breaths? I turn
around. A child air-hungry

on his hands
and knees, head

bowed by the gallery
entryway. The boy

is choking on
smoke, on
toxins, on

Vesuvius glowering.

MEDITATION ON SURVIVAL

a heron stalks by the window
and dewdrops form on grass

a smattering of light this
sweat-soaked august

lavender bedroom walls melt
like a slow day's sunset

into pain's incessant
and insistent gray

a softened sand dollar
or mangrove trees

with their tangle of roots
in endangered sand dunes

a rainbow arches above
the ocean—everything

is improbable

ADOLESCENT SEA TURTLES REST IN THE BAY

a daily life where, somewhere,
a loggerhead snacks on sponges

while she cruises through coral,
her own version of carb-loading,

the energy for always surfacing.
Who thought it was a good idea

for anything that breathes air
to live in water; always near

the surface. Holding our
breath takes work, though I wish

I could close the lid on my lungs
for a few hours a day, sink

to a shallow inlet, elbows holding
my body in place between pylons.

WHAT THESE NIGHTS SHOULD HOLD

In evening's falsetto, spilled coffee grounds
look like the swarm of ants I sprayed,

a caramel dripstain like the sun's corona
peeking out behind the carafe. Last year,

I went to bars and timed miles of broken lines
from Birmingham to Gulf Shores before winter

sputtered into the summer of walls and walls and
still: a sliding glass door leading to a reservoir

of afternoon mosquitoes, rippled amber sunsets
hardly worth the bite, a sky matching the whiskey

I shiver down my throat. It's too cold for ants
this time of year. Bars feel fiction, now far removed

from some December's felt and bluechalk pool
shots. I glass myself another, swipe counters clean.

The dishwasher gears slam. I swear
I hear an eight ball's break from blocks away.

HOME SAFE

Even tornadoes are worthy of our full
attention, a type of worship. Their swirl
seductive, and green skies make a jealous

wreck of everything the twister steals:
bicycle tires, rakes, washrags, a metal roof,

car seats, tree limbs, and photographs—all

dropped into the river, sent careening;
eventually caught on a stranger's porch,
collapsed over a farmhouse's old frame

towns away from here, where the birds
shake loose the damp from their down,

and beak the seeds closest to the dirt's

surface, their nests still between tree
limbs. Our bodies turn like sunflowers
to the noonday light. We share in our

delight with the endless flurry of bees,
their low hum of excitement, torsos

plump as they shake off excess pollen.

FOREST BATHING

Undergrowth in the spotlight. Geometric
stripes of sun fan out from the clouds

like the fingertips of some god. Geosmin.
And mushrooms as if from nowhere.

A rat snake, its home surely flooded,
scans for dry with its ancient tongue.

Shoves of wind wring loose rainwater
from the forest canopy. Lichen glows

cream and green on peeling bark. A flurry
of squirrels hold home in a stand of pines,

their needles the burnt umber of an early
autumn. Nature makes it look easy,

all this dying. Staying still. The waiting
for leaves to drop. Finding another way

to make use of what's already gone.

PORTRAIT OF THIS MENTAL SYMPTOM AS JEOPARDY! CLUES

For an insured emergency therapy session:
This mental symptom, which scientists now believe is often found in Complex-PTSD, is defined as "feeling detached" from self and/or others.

For reorienting a new therapist:
During *this*, listed in the DSM-VI as a symptom of a disorder of the same name, sufferers may need a way to anchor back into their corporeality.

For engaging in conversation with friends:
When experiencing *this*, people often report feeling like their arms and legs aren't theirs; like they're doing daily tasks, such as making coffee, on auto-pilot.

To not hyperventilate in public again:
Often a sign that someone is having a c/PTSD flashback, *this* series of disarming symptoms begins without warning and can result in a panic attack.

To finally feel at home in my own bones:
If they can recognize symptoms of *this* phenomenon before it starts, some re-orient their reality by engaging in grounding exercises, such as meditation or a bath.

[Answer: What is dissociation?]

THE KING HAS CANCER

Thin as a papercut, but no one will say
so. Wasting away, even. Whispers of his
status in every corner, and few are sad.

On the lawn, a child rolls snowballs taller
than she is, stacks them one by one. Plucks

red berries for eyes. Fashions a crown of dead
hickory and hornbeam leaves, and places

it on the snowman. With a stick, she carves
a hammer on its chest, and practices a series
of runes she is years away from understanding

beyond their clunky and humanly meanings:
a day, gods and giants, wealth, ice, ulcer.

The farmers show up in pods, say our food
supply is running low. They need water.

Everyone needs to eat. But the King has
chemo. And doesn't it seem that everyone
is sick these days? But it's not a question.

The Queen is in the cupboard, tongue
pressed to a pill she wills herself to swallow.

A COMING OUT POEM THAT ENDS IN JOY

On the other side
of my nana's kitchen window,

hummingbirds sip nectar
from a trumpet vine

and I know her forest-yard keeps her
sane in seasons when surprises

pile up in the sink like spoons
and when I finally tell her,

it is long after the hydrangeas
turn paper white, drop to dirt.

She tells me she saw a mama deer
birth twin foals last week,

that she calls them sweetie—
that she knew the whole time.

HOTTEST SUMMER ON RECORD

Even the ferns are sad, fronds curled
and panting under our livid sun. No
amount of water can parch the thirst
of this swollen drought. In the lake,

warm as a tepid bath, we toe the mildew's
thrive on the rocks under our toes, but at least
the fishes and snapping turtles stay tucked
away. Despite our relief, we can't help

but worry about them. We whisper. It is still
beautiful here. The lake's surface smooth
enough, stones would scatter the quiet,
ripple the corals and teals and moon rising

in the sky's reflection between us as if we're
the last two on our planet. We may as well be
to the dragonfly hunting in the pier's shade,
its metallic green eyes almost molten when

the light hits. To the wild hare resting in red
dirt under the azalea bush. To the caterpillars
praying under their leaves that tomorrow will
still manage to wake up. I want to cup water

in my hands for them all. Want to wade
through my disappointment. Pull myself
dripping onto the dock. Crack open an orange
to offer, like anointment, a lap of sweetness.

DEFINING WHO I AM BY WHAT I REALIZED I'M NOT

The first time I saw her nails long
and painted blue, chipped with cheap
polish from my undergrad backpack—

days when I cinched my long hair up
high and tight, always out of my face—

she wore a floor-length dress fresh off the hanger
and I could see every joy she'd ever hungered
for green in her irises, shiny as hatchlings

racing for the water in a euphoria
we each hope for the chance to feel.

I watched her spin and spin, dress ebbing at her
ankles like an arc of saltwater designed to heal
bodies like ours, carapaces fresh and uncalloused.

IN WHICH THE DOOR IS A METAPHOR FOR DIAGNOSIS

The first girl pulls her sweatshirt's sleeve over her wrist. The other
frees a slipping scrunchie loose from her hair and re-twists it into

a bun. Business as usual. Wheel the kegs into the cooler. Unwrap
the stacks of lids from their plastic. They've known each other

for years, in this same back room of a downtown hipster
eatery: part coffee shop, part bar. Walls aggressively green.

It's unclear what has come before: if they have just had sex
or if they always look askew and flushed. She clicks the pen,

tucks it into the other girls' Nickelodeon-orange apron, which comes
across as an excuse to pat her chest where a logo reads: *Pluto—resist labels.*

As loud as waking under invasive lights, a phone rings from the other
side of what can only be described as an unsuspicious door.

NEW DIAGNOSIS: CYSTIC FIBROSIS RELATED DIABETES

Blood sugar high enough she should (by the way
the nurses are looking at her) be in a coma. She says
the IV feels like fire ants in her veins. The nurse in blue
scrubs doesn't think the child sees her roll her eyes,
but of course the girl does. It will be a week in

the hospital, where the girl and her mother learn to give
her insulin. Four shots a day. They learn to count carbs,
which the body turns to sugar. For the next year—at least—
they measure out orange juice in half-cups. This is not what
twelve was meant to look like. Every snack becomes cheese

and pecans and grapes by the handful. She is angry
at the world, herself, her parents—that something as plain
and necessary as eating freely is taken from her. Eventually
she will learn forgiveness; accept this is no one's fault.
That whether or not it's fated, it is what it is. This is her

responsibility. Still, as many times as she's told, it will never
get better. Or easier. It's simple for others to ignore the lifelong
complications she will likely face: nerve damage, kidney failure,
blindness. Every day, all these adults around and it's up to her
to carry the weight of knowing what will eventually take her life.

INJECTION TRAINING

On the overbed table: a pile of ketchup
packets, a baker's dozen of straws

brought with each new Styrofoam cup
of ice water or juice or sprite, cannulas still coiled,

open pouch of syringes, cyan stressball,
alcohol wipes in foil houses. The nurse's hair

shimmies like late October leaves. *Practice.*
Hold the syringe like this, she instructs,

pinching one of them between first knuckle
and thumb flesh. In her other hand, the ball.

We mime her squeezing blue foam fat.
This is your stomach, she tells us what we see

on TV is wrong–not to ready thumb on plunger,
use our index finger. No sensationalism. No dramatic flair.

After, a dewdrop of insulin leaks from the hollow
needle. Plastic clicks on walnut laminate.

NIGHT COYOTE AT THE OCEAN'S EDGE

with moongone sky
with endless sea
with sightblind fog:

sepia eyeshine

a wolfhound god
a cloudbound blur
a shadow's shade:

hazy pepper coat

the footfall hush
the luckstruck view
the lunghold gaze:

battlebound and beastbred mist

then pawprint coast
then southern breeze
then cloudless sky:

ceramic starshine

and salttrimmed crabs
and spearblade light
and gulfpink fins:

sunrise of another kin

HER HAMINGJA

from Old Norse mythology, a female spirit who resides within each person's Self and determines luck. Believed she could be 'lent out' to others, though the gift was not always consciously given or received

her crib	her thumb	her lungs
the Vejle	the coast	the fjord
her hope	her heart	her heave
to rose	to grove	to mauve
her sight	her sickle	her siege
the heron	the eagle	the raven
her fog	her fates	her flame
to ghost	to ghost	to ghost

AUBADE WITH SWAMP SOUNDS

The world is made of insects
and amphibians searching
for each other in the dark

and moon-mad morning. All
animals wake up hungry or horny.
Or both. Full out cacophony of legs

playing on each other like a violin,
throats like tambourines, a thorax
that makes all the cicadas jealous.

Is it the excitement of desire
or the hope for mere moments
of satisfaction to come that sings

us all into daylight? The calm knowing
that eventually we will find each other—
all spindly legs or branch-grazed wings.

TODAY IS THE COLOR OF A STANDARD HOSPITAL-MASK

Not unlike the tenth floor's
in-patient walls, and I think
of the faceless contractor
stepping outside for a better

look at a paint chip It feels
obvious to me he must have
tried to pick a cheery shade
for some silly reason. The color

of sky, because some of us aren't
permitted to leave our rooms. Or
because bulk discount. Or because
there are children in here and no

need for the metaphor to be deep—
the whole day may as well be washed
in sky. Cold blue. Water that, like potential,
goes on forever. A fluorescent

and blinding blue that always puts
me right back there. In a folding bed.
Soap operas and endless gameshow
television. Third set of labs this morning.

Sterile air in spring. Green willows and pink
tree-blooms eclipsed by a surgical lighthead.

SURGICAL THEATRE

my body slab-flat on a metal table;
my jaw pulled toward the ceiling;

my tongue held to make room for the rigid
tubes in my throat. Nurses swaddle my legs

in warm blankets simply because I said I'm cold.
Straps secure across my thighs because feral

when unconscious, survival brain will try to keep
anyone out. But I signed the forms for anything

that goes wrong or right for the hours I am
given to the professionals reaching into my chest.

They cradle pieces of my flesh and bone. They know of me
what I never will: the color of the inside of my lungs;

the sound a wheeze makes with my larynx exposed;
the crippled state of my blood before it reaches the heart.

IMPORTANT INFORMATION ABOUT YOUR BRONCHOSCOPY

after what is supposed to be an outpatient procedure

crinkle rose pink
speckled gunk-spit
into a tissue,
ribcage rattling
from bronchi in full bloom;
tastes like pollen-dust
scratchy, stuck
in chest
that won't
let go of sludge
no matter how much
air exists,
crunching muscle
against muscle;
from a sterile room
watch a city crow
cast aside a plastic straw,
in full control of what
goes in his throat.

WHEN COUGHING RUBS MY THROAT RAW

My voice missing.
Vocal cords swollen

purple and heavy
as a pocket of stones.

Words fall from a hole
in my throat. My lungs

shimmer green slugs
and clumps of feathers

up my windpipe
from lower bronchi;

make their way
to the true center

of my chest, tickling
raw muscle until

I cave to the sharp
beak pecking

the apple cramped
behind my larynx

with a rib-cracking
hack I at least know

to brace against:
squeeze arms to

my barrel chest.
The gagging starts.

Supposedly I'm lucky,
just a cold... but still, I

beg these barn swallows
to find some other lobe

of mud to nest.

BRONCHOSPASM

I.

the dead air between
breaths. from ancient
Greek; broncho- as in

a gland or lymph node,
-spasm as in a violent
and painful noun. not

always, but sometimes
fatal. usually associated
with an underlying cause.

adjective of convulsion.
the word as old as lungs.
a heaving, natural force.

II.

no
in- or

ex-

hale
caught

mid-

cough
in a

breath

between
in-

and
wonder-

ing if

air
will

if carbon
dioxide

will

my
bronchi

to let
in

breath

like
knives

past

this
muscle

I (must

sit)

am
spasm-

dizzy
to

inhale
oxygen

EACH NIGHT, I WAKE IN THE WITCHING HOUR

Thin blue plumes of smoke
float above the surface
of the water;

in my stomach, a shame
bubbles up from
canvas-white

panic. I measure the wingspan
of my emotions as if
I don't know

chirping wrings this night of its long
and wilting moon—a tune.
Without words,

I will end up overwhelmed—
choking on feathers
when all I see

is dwindling lung capacity in fog,
an inhaler always primed
on the bed.

BAD MOON ON THE RISE

We order our BBQ cheeseburgers at the counter
and meet at the corner booth in the window
to watch the crowd of freshmen jaywalking
in the rush between classes. Sweet tea refills

beside the coke machine. Straws to the left.
Order up; queso fries. Smiles on the sidewalk,
both wilted and blooming. Phones on phones.
A backpack pocket blissfully unzipped. Extra salt

on the tortilla chips; doctor's orders. Two tables down,
businessmen talk golf. Fried catfish on a passing plate.
Ketchup stuck like glue to the sides of the bottle. Pass
the pepper. If you want, I'd go in with you on dessert.

A handful of plastic spoons. Swap the empty napkin
dispenser for the full one no one's using. Someone
turns up the volume on Creedence Clearwater. This
much grease might kill us all, but who cares?

THE OPPOSITE OF FEAR IS TRUST

When I was still young, I thought the trees
at the end of my parents' street came alive
each night. That every tree branch was a snake
waiting to reach down and pluck the bike

helmet off my head. That a cup of orange
juice could really boost my immune system
enough to keep me out of the hospital. That
the sun welcomed each morning's long and

slow stretch into sky as much as anyone does
the day's first yawn. Today, on an isolated
mountain road, freshly single and the Cumberland
Gap between us; I learn how to feel my hands

touch the earth and feel anything besides hurt
again, I found myself afraid of every possibility:
of a scorpion under each rock, of rattlesnakes
waiting in every pile of autumn leaves to fang

my foolishly exposed ankle. What I'm saying is,
I've always lived my life on a razor's edge,
always sure the next moment ready to
crosshatch blood from the arches of my feet;

but the water that springs from these mountains
is the most naturally pure on earth, or so I read
somewhere. I hold my shoes, wade through
the creek, and wait for nothing bad to happen.

IF I FORGIVE MYSELF, TODAY'S GENDER CAN BE ANYTHING

a great blue heron sunning wings-wide
on a broken pier or a clematis vine covered
in whirligig baby bulbs. a deer complacent

with losing its spots. a stump speckled with moss
and mushrooms. a line of red ants with a feast
over their heads. a sun's aluminum reflection

off the lake. a day slow with that salty kind
of humid, like a curling edge of willow bark.
a hydrangea's snowball-bloom wild and thriving.

THE NORNS

teeth and hair. veins
and the grain of our skin.
blood type. viruses. back

pain. wreck of nerves.
hand shape and size and
oxygen's vulnerable tanks.

love calling it quits. a tree stump
will never be what it once was.
full of the wild. heavy with leaves.

a home for blind snakes.
toxic mushrooms. invasive
beetles. wisteria allergy.

grass pollen flare. what
it feels to know of the rain's
coming by my swollen knees.

UBI SUNT FOR HATCHLINGS AND THEIR MOTHER

Un-retractable
flippers paddle wet on sand,
sound lost in ocean's

crash that spits her out
in front of us. Dark shadow
sliding slow, a sloth

tethered to high tide's
gravity, she feels for dunes
under her chin. Stops.

Back legs dredge a hole
beneath her. Fifty-three whole
minutes. We see her

maternal muscles
shiver instinct, a prayer
to the moon. Her clutch

of eggs now separate
from her for good, she frenzies
a sand tornado

to protect these gems
from a world she can't control.
She moves faster now

than her trek inland,
pains settled and the shore sloped
toward the ocean's tongue,

the moon's light guides her
far from coyotes and fox
and her midnight clutch.

WHAT I'D WANT MY CHILD TO CALL ME

and we're gluing glow-in-the-dark solar systems
on the ceiling; shading looping and lopsided flowers

in chalk on the driveway; cookies left open on our
counter; toys in various states of secret-project-driven

doneness on damn near every surface of the place. But,
at least I've managed to get the laundry separated. We've

filled the fridge with fresh strawberries and tomatoes and
it's summer. Three bruised shins so far doesn't stop anyone

once there's ice packs and a bowl of vanilla to ease (or at least
distract from) whatever pain the gravel or turf caused. I want

the curve of my hip to serve as a human-carrier for as long
as I can stand the weight. I'll give whatever I can to hear soft

morning babbles turn loud and angry with hunger. For tears
and snot on the collar of every plaid shirt I own, and for sugary

breath of a kid learning to take what they need of language
and call me whatever they know to mean *home* and *safe*.

IN THE GUEST BEDROOM OF MY PARENTS' HOUSE, I RUMMAGE A PHOTO OF A VERSION OF MYSELF I THOUGHT I'D LOST, AND I NEED TO SAY, DEAR GIRL:

All the time, you believe you're telling
a sad story as opposed to a safe one

and a mind possessed by evil notions
must begin stocking up with images:

and a southern sun where the milk
of a mountain laurel is toxic

and synchronous fireflies flash
an eye-blink of splendor

and spicebush swallowtails beeline
to turk cap lilies for their orange

and autumn is nothing more
than a cup of tea gone cold.

and you will not die because you are
sick but because you are alive.

and the worst thing about therapy
is the juvenile metaphors.

and not all fears are rooted
in the darkness.

and pretending the hospitals are empty
does not actually make them empty.

and a sheltered life is a daring life
when even the smoke is out to get you.

and somewhere the 52 Hertz Whale's sound
signature is plated on a scientist's wall

and goddamn, that tiny sliver of hope you
believed could fill your heart? You hate it now.

and an essential pre-requisite of a good researcher
is the willingness to be wrong

and the invitation of constructive critique.
But when you can't see something

and the doctor tells you...
you can't understand the severity.

and just because your life is a mess
doesn't mean your kitchen has to be.

and accumulation is the result
of obsession. It's Wednesday

and even mushrooms pray
to the stars. Lesson one is survival.

and you're supposed to be leaving soon,
so forgive the spring ephemerals

and the canopy that starves
them of sunshine

and alchemy rising out of the mud
of the river that sings

and save all your ghosts
for a ritual of remembrance:

your body hovering delicately
on the last edge of childhood.

IMAGINING MY MENTAL LANDSCAPE AS WILDERNESS

About the time I start to believe I am the sole cause of every unhappiness I experience, I remember context exists and pause to listen for the singing that Dickinson once called Hope, to hear only a roar of bullfrogs and a weak flutter that could be feathers, but they're deep in that bullfrog's growl, and I am sure the bird has been consumed by some other beast entirely.

MASLOW'S HIERARCHY OF NEEDS IS BULLSHIT

imagine the chronically ill body
often, but not always, on fire
flames bloom and metastasize

bone pain sharp
lung tissue constricts
throat scratched by hellhounds—

imagine the body's owner
heaving in and out of flaming
without reprieve from either the pain

or the appointments, doctors,
needles, tests that perpetuate
pain searching for answers

in DEXA and CAT scans
that rarely answer where
anyone expects

then, side effects—crippling
nausea, supernova headaches
caused by the nausea medicine

anemia from the third antibiotic
cocktail; oral and inhaled in tandem
that still don't stunt or calm

IV lines busting veins, appetite
poor, irritation, depression
imagine: all of this

without music,
without TV,
without tattoos that make

your body into
a somewhere
worth surviving

CEMETERY WALK

to imagine myself here is easy with every patch

of tri-lobed lilies and bouquets left behind of daises

and zinnias or carnations by the moundful or here

in this mangle of leaves over forgotten rests

of stone unidentifiable and worn smooth by rain

and time and shoes not unlike mine tread of

asterisks hourglass or snowflakes this time

of year the grass yellow crumpled unrelenting winter

and names recognizable for centuries on street

signs and some infants are infants forever in the

months that become no more than a space

smaller than a forehead or somewhere

to sit and contemplate the wispy passing clouds

the couples uncoupled for now and don’t the evergreens

have it easy among these roses

PROGNOSIS

offer the bedbound child
blackberries in winter.

know when she turns

over the palmful in her
hands and sees mold,

she'll try to scrape the scabs

off like barnacles from silk.
she's too young to know

better. grew up on promises

of fresh bounty all year;
of course she expects

more than this. adults say

nearly anything to calm
a terrible moment. no one

could have predicted

that the color of her panic
would forever be this purple.

PRAYER

No needles. Or, if needles,
make it painless. Shred the old
consent forms. Let there be no
side effects for skipping a dose.

Or two. No clinic follow-up,
certain in the treatment plan
unfolding just as it should.

A well-rested heart beats
steady and with enough
oxygen, it feels like anything
can turn warm. Normal.

Please let this body bring me
endurance in its decay. Comfort
despite some primal knowing:

to fan open a pine's dropped
switch in the forest will
reveal blight marbling
this once-healthy tissue.

ACCOMMODATIONS

Soup when we are sick.
Bread and ginger ale to

settle the stomach. I break
out in hives at fermented foods

(which includes beer); a new
symptom. And half-German, part

Welsh, that I am, do not yet know how
to resist sauerkraut on a brat braised in

stout. To make up for it, brine my hives
in a bath with fists of Epsom salt. Drink

plenty of water. Accept I am charted in
some past doctor's notes as non-compliant,

and years on I will learn
how disabled does not have

to mean weak; is not a bad word.
And my needs are not different

than any peer. How it's not special
to need clean air. Or to eat when

so hungry we are shaking. It is
normal to crave loving arms

wide like bare branches and
whose safety you might one day

realize you took for granted.
Like every child, I too collected

acorns in the yard. Rocks in clear jars.
Trampled my feet through the mud.

Watched leaves drop, dry on the ground
like cupped hands. Was too young

for the words to make of my body
(which hurt yes, even then) beside

the ones prescribed. Vertigo as constant
a company as the squirrels rushing from

branch to branch. Extra oxygen cannulas
draped over the banister so no one steps

on them. This is not the story of a girl
who wants to be sick; the power imbalance

or empty eyes of strangers judging her
in the grocery store, passing by an aisle

where the sounds of coughing up a lung
feel like they echo off the shelves. A boy

once told me it isn't about what we deserve,
but how else should I respond to being

called unreasonable for requesting equality?
Wait for an office to give me approval?

THERE'S A PIGPEN IN HER LUNGS

the doctor explains her infection by way of metaphor;
her amalgamation of infections have become a sty,

impossible to separate a speck of mud from a cluster
of pseudomonas cells from an aspergillosis colony and

the sound of her cilia struggling air across her chronically
over-mucoused membranes. And she supposes the wheezes

her body makes could sound like a sick hog. Her deep
breaths trigger coughing fits. To treat the fungal infection

means feeding the bacteria, as is the case with these things,
the doctor says. Unable to listen, she swallows a muddy

clump in her trachea, as if burying it in stomach acid will help.
There are sea turtles on this doctor's bow tie and she hopes one

day she can hear of her body as more than an animal in the need
of survival; the excess of salt on her skin, a constant holding her breath.

WHEN I SAY MY PAIN IS AN EIGHT, I MEAN

mouth pain daily. if I lift something
heavy and while twisting the wrong
way, my rib pops like a knuckle. yes,
it hurts sharp enough to still me. pain
is remarkable, a steady predator; demands
I be nothing more than my tense and aching.

if I could notice the sky, I'd say it ripe peach,
a robin's chest. fish in the sun. tough lessons
in life are so loud; name a situation where
urgency isn't demanding. chaos. if I trust
you with my body, know I am giving
most of something that isn't mine.

I'LL EVENTUALLY NEED NEW LUNGS

in a dream, spring arrives as a real deluge,
leaves heaving her name through the door.

night-consumed and improbably sick.

stud-stripped walls like a construction site.
spine metalcold. cotton candy pink insulation

exposed, swollen like a stomach. stars fall
in the yard, make holes in the roof

and leave behind ashy bruises on an unlucky

single night-blooming cereus. and attached to an IV pole
large as a chandelier, she drags ocean-bound.

stitches visible under the flimsy blue gown.
a broken string of pearls. tidecracked sand dollars

and the U-turn of a sea turtle's false crawl.

FROM ISOLATION

an abstract painting becomes
no more than a daily Rorschach:
a smack of jellyfish, sea spray
on dry sand, a strobing stoplight,

the shape of Iceland, freckles
on a stranger's arm, a felled
tree in the current; all running

and gravity and wearing smooth
each rock to be stacked into a cairn

beside the river, which must be tired.

IV ANTIBIOTICS AT HOME

in my bed surrounded
with buzzers

with wires with tubes
with—

a symphony of carrion
swooning

over the distant tree line
of sweetgum

of sycamore of oak of ash:
invisible—

what breathes through kudzu,
ivy, spanish moss.

JOHN LENNON HAUNTS THE HALLS OF THE DAKOTA

lonely people
on a train stop

and say hello

I want to hold yesterday

like blue
don't you know nothing is real

tangerine trees and

marmalade skies

light of a dark

black night

doing nothing but aging
living is easy with eyes closed

don't let me down

take the news

rather sad

make it better

swallow my pain people

turn away waiting for this moment

to be free

in the dead

of night

swallowing my pain

look at all

the lonely

ELEGY FOR

the slanting hill of gravel too overgrown
the raw umber of her dog's morning breath
the yellow apple dropped from the trash
the house whose boards have long come loose

the fox and deer unable to scavenge a shelter
the freckles spanning her range of forgiving knuckles
the rusted bumpers, all the rotten roots
the forest eroding beside a dead stretch of highway

GRIEF WANTS ANSWERS

Stained glass makes shadows
on the floor like betadine

on skin. There used to be
a body in my bed I could

touch, if not love. Flat
stomach I'd stare at as long

as I wanted, clear tape held
tubes in her chest I had

to learn how to change.
Pull adhesive up, not

away, for a more painless
removal. Place a warm

compress on a sore IV
to reduce pain. No crisis

is fixed in isolation, as in
we understand solidarity

as verb. Our plates full
of green and savory

sustenance tended
by hands we'll never know.

A TICKLE IN HER THROAT

and this almost-girl learns to swirl a spoon
 through a brew she's thinned to last her through thaw
as if she can hold a bowl of health in her hands again,
 for the first time since some other life she just knows
from dreams. mid-night growls in the rose bush
 on the out side of her blinds. trouble in this place
she once called home. this body she once knew
 could out-run any bear now a cage of scared bees.
she sees his brown paws shake last night's trash
 out on the porch from her spot by the sink
where she hopes to fend them off
 with the bone broth that blooms
on the stove. more magic
 than the meds when this type
of rage stings her lungs
 and she senses wolves
stalk the woods'
 for their own share
of what
 might be
left
 over

AN APPALACHIAN TIGER SWALLOWTAIL

swoons in figure eights
over my head.

we're all just trying
to find some peace

from spring's endless rain
flooding thin creeks

into whitewater
rivers, ready

to carry away
yesterday's fresh

limestone and silt
that thundered loose

and downhill
to where tree-cover

balms summer's hottest
unrelenting wither

and her black-striped yellow
wings luminesce.

FROM MUSCLE SHOALS TO MOBILE

Travel the rhythm of the Tennessee
river away

from its open mouth: past a litany of repetitive
Birmingham billboards;

past the peach park in Clanton; past
"Go to church or

the devil will get you!" Past the Montgomery
actors playing fools

and kings, skulls in hand; through our delta,
past the point

where medians of pines turn waterlogged cypress.
And keep south

until the road ends at Alabama's best kept secret:
long stretches

of beach white as sugar. Where, if craned the right way,
you can watch the barges

come and go and wait starboard. Everything bows to what
must remain navigable.

Traffic stopped, while on the radio, a small rain
of piano

into voice low as a heron hunting smooth and
steady. Contralto

into bass; and to hear it, go and sit in a slough;
quiet, save

only the annual cicadads and ordinary
people in their yards,

lawn mowers spitting shreds of grass
over their seawall—

kudzu vines up to your elbows and wait
long enough:

you'll hear the music in the sway
and swing

sway and swing, sway of water never
ceasing.

ODE TO THE GREEN FLASH

I lose count the hours waiting
for the seemingly endless sun
to wade into the gulf. Sometimes,
or whenever possible, I focus on
biting winter, how impossible
tastes like euphoria or freedom;

a key lime bright as channel markers
in Mobile Bay, intense as boat fires.
Sometimes, or whenever possible,
I remember not to blame myself
for the natural wanting to hold
constellations on my tongue

like any normal person does
each night. I walk the disappointed
shore and try not to stare at the sun,
hoping for the horizon to flashbulb
into this night. Seafoam in my cupped
palms, I listen, when possible, to amber
bubbles as if a handful of champagne.

RECALLING A DREAM OF STRAY CATS EVERYWHERE

on the chaise
on every counter
on bookshelves

reaching for doorknobs
talons in tables
my memory like fever

little else besides the sheer number of cats
that the more I looked around whatever dark
anxious space it was the more and more cats

of every color... though most were just variations
on calico. and no noise, just cats.
and when I tell you about it, I know you will ask me

what else there was. and listen:
who's to say what all these cats are a metaphor
for-clinic appointments to corral

then endure, or insurance bills I must organize,
or my own psyche spread out across every corner
of my apartment like my laundry I still need to wash,

or shirts and socks themselves waiting for me to pay
attention to them. all I know is, I stood in some liminal
space with every cat in the world. and was responsible

for them all at once; if you were there (I can't say for certain
that you were) you were the cat with one grey eye. and I don't
know about you but I haven't felt human in a long, long time.

ACKNOWLEDGEMENTS

Thank you to the editors of the publications in which the following poems first appeared, sometimes under different names, or in different forms:

Armstrong Literary: "Injection Training"
Asheville Poetry Review: "From Muscle Shoals to Mobile"
Birdcoat Quarterly: "The Opposite of Fear is Trust"
The B'K: "Important Information About Your Bronchoscopy"
Blood Orange Review: "A Coming Out Poem that Ends in Joy"
Booth: "Recalling a Dream of Stray Cats Everywhere"
Citron Review: "A Tickle in Her Throat"
Complete Sentence: "Each Night, I Wake in the Witching Hour"
Ecotheo Review: "Aubade with Swamp Songs"
Gulf Stream Literary Magazine: "The Girl with a Pearl in Her Wrist"
Hellebore: "Portrait of This Mental Symptom as Jeopardy! Clues"
J Journal: "Ode to the Green Flash"
Porter House Review: "Sixty-Five Roses :|: Cystic Fibrosis"
South Dakota Review: "In Which the Door is a Metaphor for Diagnosis," & "Imagining my Mental Landscape as Wilderness"
storySouth: "Elegy for What These Nights Should Hold"
SWWIM: "Surgical Theatre"
Texas Review Press Alabama Anthology: "Another Type of Hospital Room," "Night Coyote at the Ocean's Edge," "In the Guest Bedroom of my Parent's House, I Rummage a Photo of a Version of Myself I Thought I'd Lost, and I Need to Say, Dear Girl:"
Understory: A Zine by Loblolly Press: "Catastrophizing in a Catastrophe," "Forest Bathing"

“ **In the Guest Bedroom of My Parents' House…**” is composed of language scavenged from the works of: Emily Cinquemani, Chris Stapleton, Frances Ponge (trans. Joshua Corey & Jean-Luc Garneau), Eudora Welty, Kevin Wilson, Alex Ibe-Cumba, Yayoi Kusama, Taylor Swift, and F. Scott Fitzgerald along with several documentaries about the earth, whales, mushrooms, and Muscle Shoals, AL.

GRATITUDE

No writing project is ever a wholly isolated endeavor. *Of Water Never Ceasing*, throughout various stages of its life into this final form, would not have been possible without the support and encouragement of the following people and communities:

Loblolly Press, particularly Andrew Mack, for giving my manuscript a home. I'll never know how I lucked out in landing such a spectacular publisher and collaborator for my debut collection. Thank you, thank you, thank you.

I'm indebted to all my brilliant mentors and teachers at the University of Arkansas MFA Program in Creative Writing and Translation, where the bulk of the poems in this book started and developed. With deepest appreciation to my poetry mentors: Davis McCombs, Geffrey Davis, and Rebecca Gayle Howell. And a special shout-out to John Duval, whose Dante in Translation class influenced the early conceptual trajectory of this book, and who introduced me to what would become the epigraph of this book. How fortunate my work is for your always insightful and clever guidance.

This book couldn't have happened without the scientists and doctors who developed and provided access to life-extending and quality-of-life-changing medications and medical advancements. Special thanks belong to the doctors and nurses who showed up to my appointments ready to listen with radical empathy, and who understood that patients are always the experts of our own bodies.

My friends and community members who have provided advice and feedback throughout the process of making this book into what its become: samm binns, Jane Blunschi, H.M. Cotton, Brody Parrish Craig, Karli Drew, red nesbitt,

John Saad, Lauren Goodwin Slaughter, Mar Vincent Stratford. Whether you provided feedback on some version of a draft, or offered advice during the publishing process, thank you for being a part of this book's creative evolution.

To my closest community of COVID-conscious comrades, who have held me through some of the hardest realities throughout the creation of this book. Especially to: Adrian, Amina, Chris (AKA DJ Pastor Rock), Heidi, Jennelle, Jo, Julia, and Willow—for your commitment to solidarity as a verb. But most of all, for your consistency, support, and love over time.

Most of all, I am grateful to my parents. To my dad, for being the family pitmaster and designated 'Meat Man' and for your reliable, consistent, and safe presence. And to my mom, for always being my number one advocate and artist's assistant. But, above all, to both my parents for encouraging me to follow my artistic inclinations, because everyone has to do something; so we may as well spend our energy doing what makes us feel the most fulfilled. Thank y'all for always making sure I have a soft place to land.

Loblolly Press is an independent press based in Asheville, North Carolina. We publish contemporary poetry, short fiction, and novels rooted in the American South.

Our work is shaped by a simple commitment: sustained editorial care, long-term partnership, and making real room for voices too often sidelined elsewhere. We seek writing with a distinctly Southern register, attentive to the pressures of living here now, and grounded in communities and experiences not always represented in traditional publishing.

We exist to expand what Southern literature can hold, and to build the kind of literary home where readers recognize themselves and feel closer to the work and to each other.

RECENT AND FORTHCOMING FROM LOBLOLLY PRESS

If Lost · Clint Bowman (2024)

Distant Relations · Cheryl Whitehead (2025)

Beasts of Chase · Andrew Mack (2025)

The Computer Room · Emma Ensley (2025)

Proud Roads · Kelly Riedesel (2025)

Preludes & Other Poems · Earl J. Wilcox (2025)

Habitats · Garrett Ashley (2026)

Of Water Never Ceasing · Kristin Entler (2026)

Slow Fire · Spencer K. M. Brown (2026)

Headings set in Clother. Text set in Cormorant

www.ingramcontent.com/pod-product-compliance
Ingram Content Group UK Ltd.
Pitfield, Milton Keynes, MK11 3LW, UK
UKHW022006190726
13853UKWH00004B/1772